# Corsica
## Mare a Mare Nord

Stephen Platt

www.leveretpublishing.com

**Corsica: Mare a Mare Nord**
First published - August 2023
**Published by Leveret Publishing**
56 Covent Garden, Cambridge, CB1 2HR, UK

Statue-menhir of U Scumunicatu, above Cargese

ISBN 978-1-912460-53-3

© Stephen Platt 2023

All rights reserved. No part of this publication may be reproduced, stored in a retrieval system or transmitted in any form by any means, electronic, mechanical, photocopying, recording or otherwise, except brief extracts for the purpose of review, without the written permission of the publisher.

# Corsica
## Mare a Mare Nord

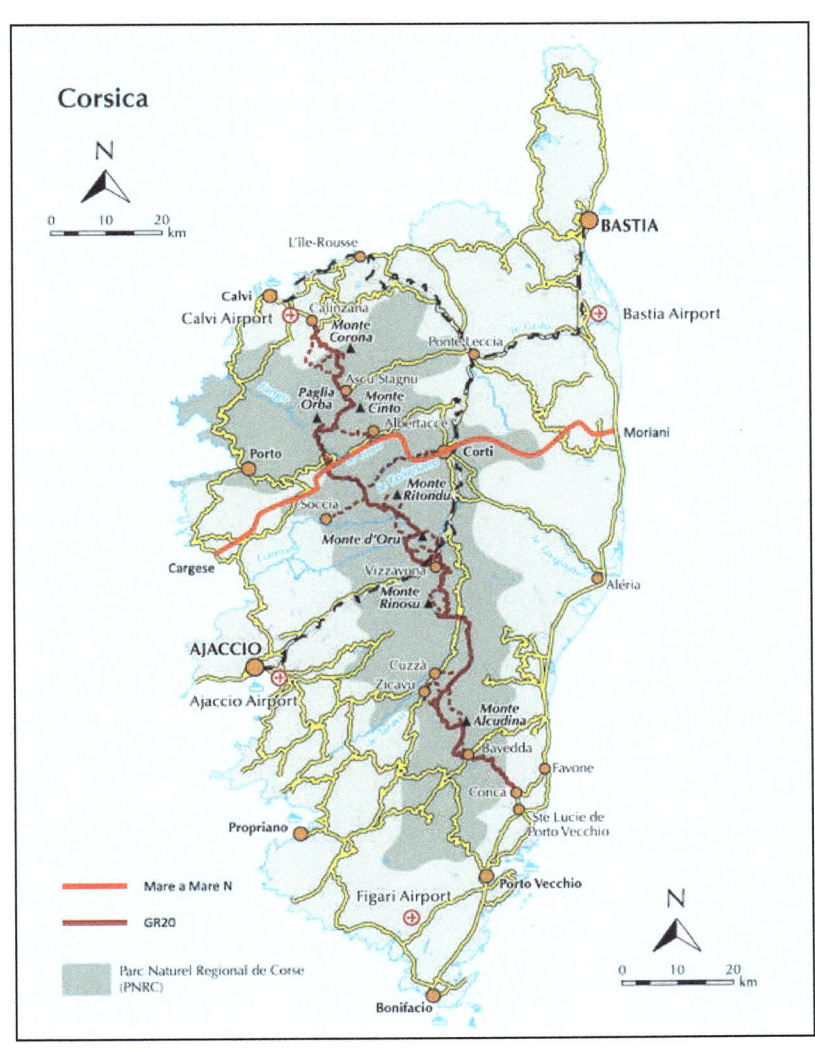

# Train and Ferry

**Friday 2 June and Saturday 3 June**

I started doing long distance walks during the Covid lock-down and thought of returning to Corsica to do the Mare a Mare Nord. I was here in 2001 and 2004 doing the GR20 and found it tough. The Mare a Mare is shorter and possibly a bit easier, but there would still be a lot of up and down. I am twenty years older; would I be able to do it?.

I'm spending a night in the hotel California 200 metres from King's Cross station because I have to be at the Eurostar terminal in St Pancras soon after six. It's a beautiful sunny evening with a gentle northerly breeze. After getting to my room I walk over to Mountain Warehouse in Tottenham Court Road to buy a towel. They have a large microfibre towels that pack small. I bought a nice purple one. On the way back I'm attracted by the sun shining on the tables of a wine bar and get a stool at the bar and order a meal.

*10 Cases Bistro, Endell Street, London*

An early start about five and the short walk to the already crowded station where it's standing room only. Seats come free after they call the Paris train. I'm taking the Brussels train and will change at Lille rather than Paris since it's just a short walk between stations.

Hurtling along in the comfortable train France seems so empty compared to England – green and well wooded.

In Lille I find a cafe and order a coffee at a sunny restaurant opposite the station. A foray to Marks & Spencer's in the station concourse to buy lunch and then the TGV to Marseilles. Near Avignon we enter limestone country. It's drier and has a Mediterranean feel to the vegetation. The mighty Rhone has embankments and drainage canals either side.

It is warm and sunny in Marseille and I decide to walk to the ferry, but when I get to the docks I can't find where to check in. No-one I ask seems to know and I end up walking too far along the front and have to retrace my steps. I see people with packs going through a gate and follow them. A shuttle bus says ferry central so I climb aboard. But when we eventually get going it sails past the Corsica births and the driver takes us to a large cruise ship at the very end of the docks and I realise I've made a mistake. After some discussion he agrees to drive back but despite my entreaties he drives past a large Corsica

*Euro Terminal Lille*

*Lille Flanders Gare*

*Le Napoleon, Cafe Bar, Lille, waiting for train to Marseille*

> **Ajaccio**
>
> Capital .of the collectivité territoriale de Corse since 1970 and birthplace of Napoleon in 1769.. Possibly founded in the 2nd century by Greeks., now with Bastia, the economic, commercail and adnminstrative centre of Corsica with about 90,000 inhabitants. It is now an importatnt stop-over for Mediterranean cruise ships.

Ferries ship that has Ajaccio painted on its bows and drops me back where I started. There's nothing for it but to walk the mile or so back and hope that's the right ship. By now my hip is hurting and I'm stressed, worried I'm going to miss the ferry. There's a high fence between me and the boat. A girl directing traffic comes over and I explain and she calls a boss who drives over, collects me and jovially whisks me to the ferry where a pretty Ukrainian girl issues my ticket, cabin key and meal ticket. What a relief! A shower and then the delicious meal in the ship's restaurant. Looking back towards Marseille I can see the huge limestone cliffs of the Calanques bathed pink in the evening sun. Bed with paracetamol for my hurting hip.

*The Calanques seen from Marseille as we leave port*

*Ajaccio harbour at dawn as we dock*

*Cargese beach seen from beginning of the walk*

**Cargese**

Cargese was established in the 17th Century by immigrants from Greece who were escaping control by Ottoman Turks. Threy came from a peninsula in Greece not dissimilar to the headland of Cargese. They prospered and perhaps because there were 11 monks, 5 priests and a bishop amongst the 500 colonists they built or restored seven small chruches in neighbouring hamlets.
Over the years they suffered attacks and persecution from Corsicans who resented their presence and had at various times to take refuge in Ajaccio. Like most other places in Corsica Caragese suffered large-scale emmigration in the 20th Century. The economy is now based on tourism.

*Hotel Restaurant St Jean, Cargese*

# Day 1 Cargese to Lozzi

**Sunday 4 June, 11km, ascent 700m, descent 700m**

I'm woken rudely by the ship's intercom, playing a Spanish song and telling me to get up because we're docking. I haven't slept well, havinghaving had a wakeful night with my hip.
Ajaccio, the port where we've docked, is on the west coast and is the capital of Corsica and the birthplace of Napoleon. It's pronounced quite differently in French and Corsican, which is confusing at first. The town is in a bay backed by mountains, some still with vestiges of snow.

There's a short wait while passengers negotiate the stairs to the car deck, then a short walk to a taxi rank outside the Chambre de Commerce and Terminal Maritime. A huge cruise liner is docked here and the passengers who can bear to tear themselves away from their cabin suites are venturing forth on guided trips into town. I talk to a couple from Montana. It's her 40th birthday and as a special treat she and her husband are taking a Mediterranean cruise.

*Plage de Peru, Cargese*

They too need a taxi, to take them to the airport to see if they can get a short flight to Corte and back before the ship leaves at 5pm. It's still early, but it seems ambitious.

A phone call to the taxi firm and a short wait then Anton arrives in a white Mercedes to drive me an hour and a half to Cargese, north up the coast and the start of the walk.

We drive through maquis – holm oak, oleander, bougainvillea, wild fig and sumac and Anton drops me outside the hotel St Jean where I'm staying tonight. A scream of 20-30 swifts are scything through the sky over the houses of the village.

The receptionist, Sandrine, is delightfully accommodating. It is still early but she lets me into the room and makes me cafe au lait and a light breakfast before I set off on the Mare a Mare path – the start being at the monument just outside the hotel.

The plan had been to walk to the refuge at E Casa and then get a taxi back from the nearby hamlet of Revinda, because the refuge was closed and there was nowhere else to stay. But being Sunday Sandrine said a taxi would be difficult. So I thought I'd walk as far as I could and then turn back and get a taxi back up tomorrow.

*Toes in the water at the start of the walk*

It's cloudy today but still warm and a little muggy. The path initially follows the steeply sloping road up the hillside then branches off on a rocky path lined with pink, purple and white Morning Glory. The rock is a grey-pink granite called schist. It was formed by metamorphosis from mudstone and shale by the same pressures that produced the Alps. The path is narrow and overgrown. It's late spring and everything is growing fast – yellow daisies, vetch, linen flax, scabious, knapweed, thistle, fennel, sage, potentilla, chickweed and heart-shaped magnolia blossom. There's the smell of herbs; butterflies and pale blue harebells, a cuckoo singing in the bottom land near the beach. and views of the sea either side of the ridge along the headline I am walking.

The guide mentioned a Romanesque chapel in ruins where the path met the road, but I couldn't see any sign of it. But I did see a phallic-shaped stone which I later learn is a menhir called U Scumunicatu dating from about 1500BC.

I was casting around for the way when a Frenchman arrived with a pack and pointed to the steep descent down a sunken lane. He said he was from Grenoble and looked extremely fit, He and his party were just finishing the Mare e Monti trek. They had camped at E Casa, which he said was abandoned. He warned me about the slippery rock and looked askance at me without poles. I said I had poles and a sack and explained about my plan for the day.

*Evening meal in Saint Jean Restaurant, Cargese*

He was right; It was treacherous. He left his pack and descended the gully with me until he reached his party. He said it felt like flying without his heavy pack.

I decided to turn back near the hamlet of Lozzi, less than half-way to the refuge because I didn't want overdo it on the first day. It seems further back than I remember – first the climb back than the descent track with bright emerald lizards and large brown speckled butterflies.

Back in my room I have a brief sleep before heading down to the sea. I buy a pear and a watermelon at the Spar over the road, which I carry in a cloth bag There's a lovely sandy beach and clear water that shelves suddenly into deep. I sit on a log outside one of the rustic beach restaurants called "paillotte", literally straw-hut, and eat the melon, and think about my very first trip abroad, to the World Scout jamboree in Marathon Greece in August 1963 where I'd had all my money and passport stolen soon after I arrived. It was my first experience of going abroad. It was high summer and scorching hot. There was no shade and I had no money to buy a slice of Karpouzi, the delicious Greek water melon.

A nice meal of poisson gratin and a pudding called Fiadone, a lemon-flavoured cheesecake made from sheep's milk followed by a difficult night on an uncomfortable bed.

*Chapel Revinda, with a commemorative plaque to WW2 resistance*

*Looking back across Revinda to Cargese*

*Looking back down heavily wooded valley of Riogna*

*Countless streams through valley of Riogna*

*Panoramic outcrop where I stopped for lunch break below Bocca Acquaviva*

# Day 2 Revinda to Marignana (715m)

**Monday 5 June, 18km, ascent 930m, descent 825m**

The taxi is coming at 8.30 and I'm up before the alarm, thankful to be moving because I had been feeling dead to the world. It's grey and drizzly outside, then thunder and a deluge. The road a river, and the roof a waterfall. Breakfast and made lunch with bread, cheese and an apple.

The storms abates and the taxi arrives. It's a Jag and the driver takes the winding mountain road much faster than I could. Revinda is small – a cluster of nine houses and a chapel. An old man is hanging about, then climbs into the front seat of the taxi to take advantage of the lift back down.

The way is easy for the first 3 km, through forest, the path is smooth, shady and leaf strewn. It's the end of spring but there still many flowers in bloom – purple Morning Glory, French Lavender, sage, juniper, bright yellow broom, chickweed and white geraniums. The path follows the valley side, crossing streams and climbing steadily parallel to the river. It steepens to reach a

*Ruined Bergeries de Casta*

*Ancient sweet chestnut trees (châtaigne); one split by lightening*

*Maybe the well-made stone path was used to carry the chestnut harvest to market*

*Climbing to the Culetta a u Prunu (970m)*

*After 2pm and rain threatens climbing to the Culetta a u Prunu (970m)*

*It began to rain soon after a stone ruin that once served as a Séchoir for drying nuts*

*Flowered slopes and rock slabs and cairn with a cross*

Cross at Bocca a u Mamucciu

The rain eases on the approach to Marignana

*Village of Marignana*

*Ustaria di a Rota, gite in Marignana*

panoramic outcrop (960m) with a view and I stop for lunch and a rest. Bergerie de Casta. The path continues to the call. The descent is stony and I trip and fall flat. It's a wake-up call, if I twist my ankle or worse it could be serious. I'm tired and I don't lift my feet and if I trip I can't correct the fall. Massive ancient chestnut trees, pigs rooting along the path and under the trees.

The guidebook says that the stone building I come to was used for drying the chestnuts and a fire was light under them all day and night to dry the nuts. The path is well made with stone blocks forming embankments in places. There are piles of manure. Maybe this was the mule train to carry sacks of chestnuts to

### Marignana

A typical Corsican village of tall stone houses built around the church of Saint James, surrounded by mountains clad in chestnut trees, holm oaks, laricio pine and floriferous maquis. The village sits astride the ancient road from Porto via the Spelunca Gorge to the Col de Vergio and on to Corte and a copper mine once provided a local economy.

*Dawn from Gite in Marignana looking west to Capu di Santa Degna and yesterday's walk*

the road at Marignana. There is a crack of thunder and the rain comes. Corsican rain is serious – it's like walking in a river. The drops are bigger and heavier than in the UK and I'm instantly sopping wet. I'm glad I put everything in dry bags since I'm not confident that the rucksack cover will keep things dry. At times it seems so wild and remote today, unspoiled. Yet clearly it's been used by mankind for millennia. The bergerie were used by shepherds' summer pasturing their flocks and the chestnuts and wild pigs are harvested. The trees look old. Many are over 3m in girth may be 500 years old.

The birdsong that has accompanied me so far stops with the thunder. There was a cuckoo sounding while I was eating lunch, but now no sound. Finally the rain eases and the birds sing again. A wooded valley with lilies and stately asphodels. A dry-stone wall and dogs barking and I know I'm reaching civilisation. And then I can see the red tiles of the houses. Past the church, which is getting a facelift, and the cemetery and finally the Gite. I'm naked in bed when a party of four French arrives.

I get up, shower, wash my clothes and sip tea in front of the fire. A large white tureen arrives at my table steaming with vegetable soup and served with croutons, followed by potato gratin, a delicious omelette, then an apple tart and cheese.

*Abandoned settlement of U Tassu (700m)*

# Day 3 Marignana to Castel de Vergio (1478m)

**Tuesday 6 June, 16km, ascent 880m, descent 120m**

I wake early and wander into the garden soon after 6. There is a deep unholy growling and I see two cats facing off at the end of the garden. Breakfast is bread and jam and strong black coffee.

The path climbs through woods to the abandoned hamlet of U Tassu (700m). There is a new roof on the church, which is open, and bells in the tower. It's interesting thinking about how people lived in these isolated hamlets away from roads and without electricity. How did the economy work? What did they harvest and where did they market what they hunted or gathered? Mules must have been the main pack animals and horses the main form of transport for people. Today you can still see mules and donkeys but very few horses.

The path drops steeply to the river, crisscrossing a tributary stream, before reaching the Tavulella River and a new bridge rather than the old suspension bridge mentioned in the guide. It's a steep climb up to the opposite bank, then

*Evisa, where I stopped for coffee at A Tramula Caffe di la Posta*

a pleasant walk along a dry-stone wall; majestic Corsican pines, potentilla, and wild rose. There are kites soaring over the road and swifts swooping over the red roofs of the houses. I climb the steep steps to the centre of Evisa and stop at a cafe near the post office for coffee and orange juice. I buy a sandwich across the road before climbing the Chemin de Chataigniers, the chestnut path. The first 200 m above the village is covered in dog crap and smells awful. But it soon clears and descends between stone walls a series of falls and pools in open woodland. A large chestnut tree is decked with bright red flags that read 'Merci'.

I meet a man who was doing the GR 20 and got to Manganu but had to bail out because of heavy rain and snow. He joined the Mare a Mare at the Col de Vergio. It's climate change he says. He has a huge pack because he's been camping. I am trying to speak French with him when I realise he's Spanish. He lives in Verona in Italy and works in tourism. I clean dishes, serve meals to tourists, he says. He seems lonely. Climate change is inevitable and unstoppable. There was no rain here from January through April, now it's too much. That's just the vagaries of the weather, I thought, but didn't say anything. All we can do is pray, he says. What about the next stage, where it would be good to camp, he asks. I tell him about the Gite in Marignana and about the ruins are U Tassu

*Lunch stop at the Piscine D'Aïtone*

*The Piscine D'Aïtone is a popular spot with day trippers*

*Wobbly suspension bridge across Tavullella River*

*Corsican pine*

*Rock pools seen from the Pont de Casterica (1186m)*

if he wants to wild camp.

The path drops down to the Piscine d'Aïtone. This is a popular spot, being near the road, with deep pools and sparkling cascades in shady woodland and there are lots of people wandering about and picnicking. I make a lunch stop on sun-bathed slabs by the side of a waterfall.

You need to cross a side stream, the rocks are slippery and I help three ladies across then step across onto a rock that is covered in 2-3 inches of running water thinking my boots will keep dry, but the right boot is instantly wet and I realise that they're finally giving out.

A steep climb out of the valley and finally an easier forest track with Laricio pine, some over 50m tall, beech and wild rose to reach a wobbly suspension bridge. It's level for a couple of kilometres and then climbs steeply up a streambed to where the trees thin and there is a traverse to the Col de Vergio. It's quite misty and there's a statue of Christ and the sound of packs of big motorbikes. Rather than descend to the GR 20 I walk along the road to the hotel, the Castel de Vergio, where I'm spending the night. The road verge is in in full flower with potentilla alba (white cinquefoil). The hotel is huge and my room is a whole suite. Dinner is a magnificent buffet with lots of choices. I am amazed by how much other people serve themselves.

*The statue of Christ in the mist at the Col de Vergio (1478m)*

# Day 4 Col de Vergio to Albertacce (860m)

**Wednesday 7 June, 14km, ascent 160m, descent 700m**

A difficult night with pain in my hip and I get only an hour's sleep between five and six. There is a long queue for breakfast but they're very efficient and people pass through quickly.

You retrace your steps back to the GR 20 and it's pleasant going through trees, following red and white flashed rather than orange. I am passed by various groups of a dozen or so people all doing the GR 20. I'm glad I'm not doing it because it looks to be very busy, quite unlike when we did it 20 years ago.

Today is all about losing height. I descend through tall stately pines and miss my way carrying on down a forest track and have to retrace my steps back to the last yellow marker to find where the trail branches off. At a military camp young squaddies are standing at ease in a circle in front of their packs for a kit inspection. There is more descent and then a climb and a traverse through

*Early start and lenticular cloud over Capu di Vergio, seen from hotel Castel de Vergio*

*Pont San Rimeriu*

*Flat stretch of shady woods*

glades of maquis with views of Monte Cinto (2706m), through clouds that are building up and threaten rain. There is very little snow from what I can see of the mountain, and it looks high.

I cross various side streams with lovely pools before reaching the main Golo River. There is a single span arched stone bridge, the Pont San Rimeriu. More downhill and I reach a second bridge, the Pont de Muricciolu, over the River Viru, with its deep pools of clear green crystalline water. It's sunny and warm and I stop for lunch and to dip my feet, wading out on a stony pebble bed of the stream. Back on the bank I dry my feet and examine my boots and find that the sole of the right boot is parting company with the upper and small stones and mud have been getting in. That's why it's been feeling so uncomfortable today I realise. My right toes are filthy.

Lizards skittering under my feet, a beautiful yellow butterfly and dung beetles. I stop and watch them pushing the perfectly round balls that are much bigger than themselves.

I find the Gite on the far side of the village. It seems closed; I'm the first there. I ring the number on the door and find that the guardienne, Dianna, is away on a medical mission to Ajaccio and will be here at 6pm. But the door is unlocked, she says, and I can go in and make myself comfortable. I shower

*Pont de Muricciolu, where I stop for lunch and dip my feet*

and wash my clothes.

I go off exploring to find a cafe, but without success as everywhere seems closed. I meet a Frenchwoman who is cycling across Corsica on a hired bike. I got a puncture, she says, but some young men helped me change the tire, then my battery died and I had to push my bike up the Col de Vergio. She seems tired but undaunted. These electric bikes are heavy without power, I commiserate. The hot sun suddenly fades and clouds threaten rain and I quickly return to the Gite. Others have arrived and say dinner is at the Restaurant Paglia Orba down the road. I go and investigate but it's all closed. Hopefully it will open later.

There's a vegetable soup and then pasta with the veal, *veau aux olives*. I leave most of the meat. Then chestnut cake and cream. An early bed. I'm worried about my boots but will try and buy glue in the next village. I get off to sleep but pain wakes me between twelve and one.

*Albertacce*

# Day 5 Albertacce to A Sega (1166m)

**Thursday 8 June, 13 km, ascent 800m, descent 450m**

Today I must regain all the height I lost yesterday. I wake well before six and pack quietly outside the dorm so as not to wake the others. For breakfast Diana has left bread and jam and I make chocolate with hot milk and am away by 7.15. My hip feels stiff walking along the pretty reservoir, the Lac de Calacuccia, but it's a beautiful morning, with blue sky, sunshine and mountains; herbs and flowers everywhere – blue cornflower and wildflowers in the verges.

There's a grocery shop open in Calacuccia that sells neoprene glue that looks as though it might work on my boots. And for lunch, I buy a bread cake with a goat's cheese gratin, a beefsteak tomato and an apple. I stop at a cafe a hundred yards further on and order café au lait and sit outside in the sunshine and glue my boots. To pay I go in and speak to an old lady sitting at the bar and give her cash and she says thank you when I wave away the change. I walk down to the dam and cross. A couple of men are strimming the long grass,

*Reservoir, Lac de Calaccia*

*Cafe de France in Calacuccia, where I repair my boots*

*Barrage (Dam) de Calacucia*

maybe to reduce fire risk around the electric substation. It seems a horrible job in the heat and dust.

The climb starts soon after the dam and ascends in a seemingly endless series of zigzags. It's stony but well-made there are flowering bilberry, bright yellow broom and Corsican euphorbia, also known as myrtle spurge. It's like a garden with endless plants and fungi I don't recognise glistening in the sunshine. I look down as I plod up the steep stony path and see that the neoprene is already stripping off my boots. It's tough and I fall over twice. It's shocking really; my legs just don't work like they used to, but I keep plodding on and by 12.30 I'm at the Bocca Arinella (1592m) and an open plateau. There's a bergerie and lots of signs of cows. The path descends and it's easy to follow the orange flashes. There is a huge slab away over to the east, rather like the Dubh slabs on Skye, when I pulled my Achilles tendon years ago and had to limp back in my wellies along the 'bad step'. I stop and sit on a rock and have lunch looking down to the Tavignano river and the E Sega refuge that I think I can see because its aluminium roof is winking in the sunlight.

I arrive early. The Gite doesn't open until 2.30 so I wander around to the water fall and the fast-flowing river. The refuge is in a most spectacular setting. The Gite opens and I make tea and have a rest. Supposedly it's an easy day

*Rock formation on climb to Bocca Arinella (1592m)*

*Bocca Arinella (1592m)*

*Gigantic slab above Tavignano Gorge*

tomorrow downhill to Corte, where I plan to buy new boots. Maybe I could get them repaired that would mean carrying them home though. Maybe these boots have done enough. We'll see.

A tall young Frenchman arrives and plonks down his kit next to the bunk opposite mine. He looks wet and complains about the rain and says he's had enough. It seems he was doing the GR20 from north to south and bailed out after Col de Vergio rather than go on to Manganu. I asked him if he came from near Lac Nino and if he liked it. He said he didn't think much of it. I remember it being the most beautiful area with herds of wild horses. Maybe we were so positive about it because it was a warm sunny day after having survived an epic the previous day when we'd been trapped in a storm between swollen rivers.

I sat with him and his new friend from Lyon who is camping. He jokes with the guardian and calls him Pasquale Paoli, after the Corsican patriot who proclaimed independence from the Genoese in about 1755. He's red-faced, full of himself and sings nationalistic songs of Corsican freedom. We're served pasta and the two young men take huge helpings. Thankfully I take only a modest amount since the main dish is followed by a rich goat's cheese and fig jam and creme caramel. A cold night in all my clothes, because they don't provide blankets here. My duvet gilet keeps me warm.

*Exploring the waterfalls near the A Sega Gite*

# Day 6 A Sega to Corte (407m)

**Friday 9 June, 14km, ascent 100m, descent 270m**

The 'Patriot' was already up when I woke at six. He must have been cold; he seems ill-equipped. Breakfast and a fast start. It's chilly, then light rain in sunshine. On these long walks songs run through your head and on this walk it's been Creedance Clearwater Revival's "Have you ever seen the rain coming down on sunny day".

The path down the Tavignano gorge is carved out of the side of the hillside high above the river, which falls in a series of cascades so you're walking with the constant sound of falling water. The edge of the path is retained by large boulders. Its ancient and well-made and goes up and down and winds round the tributary valleys. Hellebore, white and pink cistus, and cyclamen like sparkling jewels in the sunlight. I must be careful not to trip. I fell over twice yesterday. In many places the path is narrow and stony and above a precipitous drop and there would be little chance of stopping a fall of three of

*A Sega Gite in the early morning as I begin the walk to Corte*

*Having crossed the Tavignano River by the footbridge*

*One of the less precipitous sections of the path*

*Huge cliffs either side of the gorge*

*In places a trip might be fatal*

four hundred feet. I have to stop though to put a handkerchief over my neck to stop getting burnt as the sun is fierce.

There are huge, exciting cliffs on either side of the gorge. This is the centre of Corsican rock-climbing. At various points I linger a moment and pick out lines on the huge buttresses. I learn later that there are long alpine-like multi-pitch routes here, but that the main climbing area is in the Restonica gorge, the next valley south of here.

After two hours I reach a bridge over the river. Fit young people are coming up from Corte. It must be a popular day's walk to the refuge. My boots are really giving out now and I hope I can get new ones in town. Rain is forecast this afternoon, so I don't linger and there is no lunch stop today. Finally I get a view of the citadel on its greenstone rock and of terraces of ancient, abandoned vineyards.

Cherry plum trees in fruit as I enter Corte and two donkeys on a narrow path above the road. I find the hotel easily. It's closed till 2 o'clock, but the door is open, and I can dump my sack in a cupboard and go in search of lunch. I find a restaurant just down the road and order the chef salad and a beer and lemonade. It's been a hot day.

Once the hotel opens I wash my clothes and have a rest and then set off

*Rossolino Pillar, Tavignano Gorge*

*First view of Citadel, Corte*

*Arriving in Corte*

in search of boots. I find the Altiplani shop I'd seen on the Internet and tried a dozen pair, but they were all too tight. I explain to the delightfully patient saleswoman that I have bunions. Me too, she says and directs me to their sister shop next-door. I apologise for getting her running around pulling out boxes, but she says not to worry, and I touch her gently on the arm in thanks. The young man in the second shop is just as attentive. I explain what I need, and he offers me two pairs, both of which fit and feel comfortable. I buy the Sportiva pair. They're wide fitting boots and much lighter than my old leather Meindl boots and with bright pink laces that match my anorak and my current getup of pink shorts and pink T-shirt.

After a rest I sally forth to explore the town and check out restaurants that offer fish dishes. I climb to the Citadel and walk around as far as I can, then find a nice restaurant with napkins that match my new bootlaces and order a delicious marrow bone and veg soup, followed by trout and myrtle glace.

*Old boots, new boots*

*Citadel of Corte perched atop a youngish 'greenstone' metamorphic rock outcrop*

### Corte

Corte is in the heart of Corsica's mountains and was the capital of the island (from 1755-1769 under Pasquale Paoli. It's off the beaten track, friendly and quiet. Since the reopening of the city's university in the 1980s it has regained a thriving, cosmopolitan air.

The citadel is perched on a 400m high granite promontory in the centre of the town above the confluence of the Restonica, Orta and Tavignana rivers and is reached by following the narrow streets up the hill through the centre of the upper town. It was built in 1419 by the Aragonese viceroy Vincentello d'Istria.

# Day 7 Corte to Sermanu (750m)

**Saturday 10 June, 16km, ascent 1000m, descent 700m**

Breakfast and off soon after 7.30, with a stop at the Spar to buy lunch of smelly cheese, olive bread and cherry tomatoes.

I went wrong soon after leaving the town, carrying on along the main track having missed the turn off to the right. I cross fields and then an underpass that crosses the railway line. There follows a tough climb up a zig-zag path to the col and a delightful breeze. There are kites soaring in the uplift and great views back to Corte and the Tavignano Valley I came down yesterday. The path climbs to the saddle of Bocca di Civenti (785m) and another tough climb to Santa Lucia de Mercurio, where I lost the path and had to climb up through the thick prickly marquis to reach the road. A sleepy village and I stop on a bench and watch an old woman load her ancient blue Peugeot with building material and drive off with the boot wide open. There's a lovely fountain and I fill my water bottle; it's nearly empty from the climb to the col in the hot sun. Today,

*Bocca di Civenti (785m) looking back to Corte and Tavignano and Restonica valleys*

*Square in Santa Lucia di Mercurio, where I 'acquired' the orange spotted hound*

*Santa Lucia di Mercurio, perched on a hilltop, like all the villages in the area*

*Village square in Castellare, just before the rainstorm*

*Serious rainstorm – paths become rivers and downspouts become fountains*

I remembered to apply suntan lotion and to put a handkerchief under my cap to protect my neck. Nevertheless my neck feels sore.

I had been hoping to stop at the chapel of San Martinu for lunch since the weather is closing in and rain is forecast, but it's closed. I stop anyway on the high ridge, sit with my back against the chapel wall and I take off my boots and socks and rest my feet. My right foot has a memory of the stones from the last few days and feels uncomfortable. I change my socks over and it feels better.

I acquired an orange-spotted hound. It was lounging in the village square in Santa Lucia di Mercurio and now follows me as the track traverses to the next village, Castelare, which is equally sleepy.

I climb to the church square and can see rain is coming and try the doors of the church, but they're all locked. I return as the heavens open and beat a hasty retreat to an open garage at the base of the steps to the small plaza and fountain. In a second the path becomes a river, water pouring in a great arc over the parked cars from the downspout of the house in front. The hound and I are dry here in the garage.

Finally the rain eases and I climb the stony path. The dog runs ahead of me, barking and chasing cows. I yell at it to stop, but it takes no notice. We pass a succession of family cemetery plots. I learn later that Corsicans traditionally

*The orange spotted hound that came all the way to Semanu*

*Approaching Semanu*

*Parish church of the Annunciation, in Sermano*

venerate the dead and pay attention to funerary rights and burials. There is a massive open hanger that I think would be a good place to shelter. Unfortunately I've gone another mile or so when the rainstorm returns and I have to shelter under a tree, standing still trying to keep my shorts and boots dry. Finally after 30 or 40 minutes the rain eases and I start off only to be wet again by another heavy shower.

I keep to the road rather than risk the path that runs parallel to the road, reasoning that the streams will be swollen and the path muddy. The road is running with water and the streams are foaming torrents. I reach the village of Sermanu and go into the church for a ten-minute rest. On the way out a man emerges from the house in front and tells me to shut the door.

All the villages I have been through today seem empty and the few people I've see looking at me through their windows tend to pull back and hide behind curtains. This huge area, covering roughly 100km², is known as the Castagniccia. It is famous for the herds of pigs that roam the lush countryside and takes its name from the dense forests of chestnut trees (castagna). The beautiful hilltop hamlets scattered along its ridges are depopulated and many tall houses, built in the grey-green and silver schist of the region are abandoned and empty. The villages are linked by footpaths that were once the old mule tracks and this is

*Sheltering from the rain inside the church in Semano*

a walkers' paradise.

I reach the refuge after a climb up a steep muddy lane from the church. I had expected the hound to have left me by now, but it has stayed with me all day, despite looking most frustrated by my hanging around under the tree while sheltering ineffectually from the storm. Now it runs off, seeming to have completed its mission of getting me here safely. The guardian is cooking in an outside pizza oven and tells me she's expecting me and to take a bunk in Room 2.

People are already here. A man greets me with "C'est complet, haha". I'm drenched and he thinks he's being funny. Nevertheless, the other guests all seem welcoming and friendly – three women in one room, this man and his two companions in a second room and a youngish couple in my room.

I change, wash my clothes, eat the rest of my lunch and have a snooze. The rain has cleared and there is a great view across to Monte d'Oro. It's a good refuge, well thought out and there are nice people. The three women are doing the Mara a Mare the opposite way round to me. They asked me about the storm, and I said I thought it was normal for Corsica. One of the women said she came every year and had never experienced such a storm. I said I had been many years ago and there had been just such a storm. Maybe I bring the bad

*Square in Semano*

weather, I say. They asked me about my plans and mistakenly I said I was going to do the next bit in two days and then spend three days at the beach. They looked most incredulous, and I realise later that I had mistakenly thought there were only three stages to go whereas there are four.

> **Hilltop villages**
>
> The villages are built on hilltops for several reasons. The sites provided protection from enemies and pirates. The rugged terrain discouraged invaders and made it easier to defend. The mountains provided access to fresh water and grazing land for livestock. And finally, the mountains provided excellent views and a cooler climate, which made them ideal places to build settlements.

*Dorm 2 in Gîte d'étape U San Fiurenzu, Semano*

# Day 8 Semanu to Pianello (878m)

**Sunday 11 June, 13km, ascent 650m, descent 650m**

We all agreed to have breakfast at 7am. I woke early and was in the bathroom at 5.30 and soon everyone else was up. I set off and walk down the road to the village rather than the muddy gully of yesterday and find the path past the post office. The path continues down, crossing a number of swollen streams. I manage to keep my feet dry. It's muddy from yesterday's heavy rain and it is good to reach the road at Alando. The villages are strung across the hills like beads, marvellously integrated into the hillside, sitting atop rocky promontories and built with the same heavy grey granite of the local schist. They would make great weekend retreats for people from Corte, but only a relatively small proportion seem to have been renovated.

There is hardly any rubbish and no litter; such a delight after all the plastic rubbish lining the roads in the UK. The path to Alando is steep and a sign points to a panorama viewing platform. It's a 10-minute detour but it seems

*Inversion at dawn looking south-west towards Monte Cardo*

worth it. There's a narrow path which goes through the backyard of one of the houses. A father is sitting in the sun in a plastic armchair, looking after his two young children while his wife sleeps late this early Sunday morning. He waves me through.

At the viewing platform I linger looking around the 360° at mountain villages, forests and high mountains. I can see Monte d'Oro and the pass at Vizzavona, where we caught the train to Bastia twenty or more years ago.

The way runs parallel to the road from Alando to Alzi and onto Mazzola, and since the path looks muddy, steep and unattractive I stick to the road for 2-3 km. The villages are built on a similar pattern with a small square and fountain. I sample the water and drink from each of them.

A little further on, in Castelluccio, a lady in blue is taking the sun on her step. She salutes me in voluble French and tells me I'm about to climb to San Pancraziu. From the way she says it, it sounds tough. "Courage", she says. I'll need it; I feel tired and weak. I used to get stronger on multi-day walks but now I just seem to get tired.

It's muddy underfoot and I get my new boots mud caked. Crawling up the steep muddy gullies, I feel no more significant than one of dung beetles I've been watching, pushing my bad conscience up the steep slopes. Finally I'm at

*Looking west to the high backbone of Corsica*

*Massive ancient chestnut*

*Tozza Alando, 360° viewing platform in Alando*

*Lady in blue in Castelluccia who wishes me luck, saying 'courage'.*

*Path across sparkling mica slabs to Poggia*

the top at San Pancraziu (1020m) and find a bench to have lunch. From here it's a delightfully level woodland track through ancient chestnut woods, then beach beech with their brighter leaves. The path curves gently. Wild roses, flowers, birdsong and the mellifluous chant of the Blackcap.

I reach a large track and the guide says to cross and continue down so I follow the obvious track directly in front but there are no signs and after a kilometre I realise I have to climb back and find the much less obvious correct path that leads down to a stream crossing and a muddy climb to reach stone steps and clearing where one can see all the way to the string of villages leading down to the sea.

Poggia is the next goal and the way crosses mica slabs in a sea of wildflowers. At the village the path continues on to the next stage, but the Gite is in the neighbouring village of Pianello, that is down the steep hillside. The orange flashes have stopped but it's easy to find the way by following my nose down the zig-zig paths.

A sign on the door says the Gite is open to those who've reserved a place I'm early and have avoided the rain. I take off my boots and struggle upstairs and find my name on the door. The Guardian's most friendly and I drink a beer in the sunshine sitting outside in the afternoon sunshine and meet my fellow

*Église de Pianello seen from Poggia*

guests. A young French woman, her husband and daughter sit opposite me at dinner. They are touring by car, and he is on a mission to see his passion - ancient trees. He's been most impressed by the huge ancient chestnuts and the magnificent Corsican pine with their straight trunks rising many meters without any side branches. He says, he's been planting hundreds of trees. I'm a lumberjack he says, but I love trees and want to put something back.

*Emmanuel and Adele, dinner Pianello Gite*

# Day 9 Pianello to Pied d'Alesani (680m)

**Monday 12 June, 13km, ascent 600m, descent 750m**

Today should have been an easier day but I find it hard. I get away early without breakfast having made a sandwich the night before. You have to climb from the Gite in Pianello back up to the hill to Poggia. The paving is immaculate - fine crazy paving in the local rock. Dozens of swifts are wheeling around the church tower catching invisible insects and a scream of twenty follow me up the slope.

From Poggia the path narrows to a level forest trails through chestnuts until dropping down to a stream crossing then a wooden bridge over a torrent falling through a rocky gorge. The path climbs seemingly endless gullies muddy from recent rain. Then a delightful traverse across open moorland with views back to Poggia and views onward to a saddle (1050m). The path curves around the ridge to maintain height and turning south, then east, then north. This is the best part of the day, the ridge contouring round in a shallow curve, the mica schist glinting in the sunlight. Fire blackened chestnut trees, gaunt giants, one still

*Path through chestnut woods and wooden bridge over river Bravona*

clinging to life. Then a descent through dense woodland to the road to Perelli.

There are no signs and I cast around wondering which way to go. I pass a Scots woman who is on her mobile, having what seems a tricky conversation that involves some payment. I approach her and she asks me if I'm lost. She says most walkers seem to miss the last bit of the path down to the road and come out here where there are no signs. Her name is Ellie, and she has a lovely baby in a papoose called Elba. She says she's married to a Frenchman. They were living in a commune and working the land but a local farmer offered them a house and work, so they moved. I wonder what it's like living in a tiny village here in the mountains away from everything. She says she'll show me the way and we chat as we walk. When we reach the turn off for Perelli she says I can come up and take water from their village fountain. I say I'm okay for water and need to get on and we say goodbye. I imagine she's starved of company.

It is much further and harder than I expected to reach Pied d'Alesani. It began well on the road with a large flock of goats. It threatens rain so I stop at a chapel but it's locked so I put on my anorak. There are pigs on the road. The descent down through the woods is a poorly maintained slippery path. There are lots of shotgun shells and the most difficult going. From the next village there are concrete steps, then an indefinite path down the steep

*Fire blacked chestnut trees on traverse to the saddle (1050m)*

*Pig in the road, Perelli*

*A flock of goats, Perelli*

hillside through what seems to be the village rubbish dump. Why can't they maintain the path better I wonder. It's been so good elsewhere. It bodes ill for tomorrow when I'm trying to join two stages in one.

Finally I hit the road and a long slog into the village past a large raptor on a telegraph pole that flies off as soon as I lift my phone to take a shot. I reach the restaurant, that is disappointingly closed on Mondays. I had been dreaming of a nourishing soup for lunch and am disappointed. At the Gite is not clear what to do. I ring the guardienne, Patricia , who is delightful. She arrives and makes lunch for me from bits she has in the fridge. It's delicious. I doze for a couple of hours days and sort myself out. There's an electric fire to dry my wet clothes.

Patricia talks about the poor route today. Its recent, she says, the usual route is closed due to renovation. The restaurant opens specially for people staying at the gite and I have a nice chat with a young man from Paris, called Pierre Alexis, who is doing double stages, which is why I haven't met him until now. Pierre was in London for the World Cup and knew about Sheffield United. He said he seen a snake in the road. it was 2m long and dark green. I assume it's a grass snake.

*View from Pied d'Alesani Gite*

# Day 10 Pied d'Alesani to I Penti (626m)

**Tuesday 21 June, 10km, ascent 460m, descent 530m**

Swifts wheeling over the village as I leave. I make an early start at five with coffee with hot milk as a treat and a ham roll for lunch. I leave with Pierre Alexis who is also doing the Mare a Mare. The way begins along the road but as soon as we reach the fountain we branch right up a very steep path. Our conversation is so interesting that I hardly notice. Pierre has been working as a management consultant for a large company doing strategic planning for corporations, but he's become disillusioned and has taken time out to look for a new job with a smaller company. He wants to do something more worthwhile. The buzz used to always be about AI, now it's about climate change and how to deal with it, he says. But companies are only interested in how to mitigate risk and I'm sceptical that they are serious about reducing carbon emissions to combat climate change and are really only interested in their profit margins and the bottom line.

*Pierre Alexis, who was doing the Mare a Mare in double stages*

*Chapelle Sant Alessio, where I went the wrong way*

*The enticing ridge the was 180° wrong*

He says he is rather new to walking. His father does ultra-marathons, so maybe it's in the blood. He asks me about my walking and I say I used to rock climb and we talk about Alex Honnold and his ability to screen out fear and deal objectively with the risk. He must be either very good or very lucky, I say, since everyone makes mistakes and it only needs one when you're soloing a big wall. We talk about Kahneman and people's perception of risk and reward and how it varies depending on one's viewpoint. He's intrigued by the experiments Kahneman conducts. It's been delightful talking to him and has stopped me brooding about the ascent. He went really slowly for me but in no time we reach the chapel Chapelle Sant'Alessio (960m) where he leaves me, wanting to get back quickly to meet his friend in Moriani.

I have a rest and then follow. The spaniel that has accompanied us from the village has gone with Pierre. The wide path has recently been trimmed and there are plastic orange streamers hanging from trees marking the way. The ridge curves down delightfully through tall shrubs with views of strings of villages down to the sea. I've gone 2 km or more when I realise I haven't seen an orange flash. I feel I've gone wrong and check the guide and realise I've gone completely the wrong way. I should have realised earlier, having read the guide last night and seen that the way was high level and not down this curving ridge.

*Way to the Col diFrate Mortu (900m)*

To go on and find a road to the beach, or go back, having to climb back up to the chapel and start again having lost a good hour? I'd started out early today intending to combine the last two stages in one and reach Moriani by 3 to catch the only bus of the day to Bastia at 3.20. Now I won't have time unless I continue straight down and miss out the last stage and a half. The correct route goes Northwest; I was going south-east, a 180° wrong. Oh my! But the right decision is to go back and start again. So back up, collecting rose quartz rocks that I've seen on the way down as I go.

This detour has cost me an hour but I'm on the right route at last with orange markers. An enjoyable ridge with tiring ups and downs to the Bocca di Frate Mortu (900m) and then on to a junction with four or five signs, one commemorating a parachute drop of ammunition and arms for the resistance movement, the Maquis, during World War II.

I meet a couple who speak English. The man is in his mid to late 60s and is very fit. He says they're doing two stages and going on to Pianello. His younger redheaded companion asks me if I've come from Alesani. I say yes. I think she wants to stop there and not do two stages in one.

It's a stiff climb up a muddy hillside badly churned by pigs. I'm feeling tired but finally begin the long descent. It's easy to slip here. I reach bridge with enticing

*Crystal clear pools and cascades*

*Narrow walkways in pretty village of I Forci*

*Scola Santa Reparata class photo circa 1950, I Forci*

pools and the road to the Gite at I Penti (615m).

I pass through a lovely quiet hamlet of I Forci (605m) up complex steep walkways, then an easy road to the Gite. There are two male guardians. One is very friendly the other more abrupt. They make me a salad lunch with a glass of wine. The one with the abrupt manner comes over and has a friendly chat. They ring for a taxi. I could have stayed the night here but have booked the hotel in Bastia and can't cancel. I've blown it with the detour on the ridge and the lunch and there is no way I can catch the bus unless I take a taxi. My toes are hurting from the descent in new boots and it's forecast to rain heavily in an hour. It's disappointing though not to do the last stage.

The taxi driver is very talkative and I'm just able to understand his Corsican dialect. He drops me at a bus stop in Moriani near the beach just as it starts to rain. It rains very heavily and I find a restaurant and have pressed orange juice. Google suggests that there is a slight confusion over the time of the bus and where to wait but a man I ask says the taxi driver is right and the shelter I had been waiting at is okay. The bus comes at 3.15 so I'm glad I'm early.

I doze off on the bus. The driver drops me on the dual carriageway in Montesori I and I find the underpass to cross the road. I've strained the Achilles tendon in my left leg and find I'm limping along the road to the hotel.

*Celebrating over lunch in I Penti gite*

I Penti Gite

Hotel Spa Ostella Montesorro

# Montesori and Bastia

**Wednesday 22 June**

A rest day. First a latish breakfast and then to the beach for a dip in the sea. To get to the beach you cross the four-lane highway via an underpass and then drop down a long set of steps to the railway. You climb off the platform onto the track and then walk along the line for 400m or so to another set of steps down to the beach.
I climb back up to the railway line in time for a train to Bastia. I plan to go to the tourist office and get better information about buses to Cap Corse than I was able to get in the hotel. I was planning to go to Cap Corse tomorrow but am told there are no buses on Thursdays. It seems the shuttle only runs on Tuesdays and Fridays. So I change plans and decide to go on Friday and do a short walk and get the bus back in time to check in at the ferry at five. That means I have Thursday free and can go back to I Penti and complete the last stage of the walk if I get an early bus from Bastia.

*Railway line to Bastia*

The train is a nice way to get into town because the roads are congested and the little two wagon train takes just seven minutes. To try to avoid a similar hassle with checking in that I experienced in Marseille I decided to walk to the ferry terminal and check out boarding arrangements. The girl at the information desk is most surly and unhelpful. It's most unusual here. However, I figure where I need to check-in although no one is about and go back to a cafe on the promenade near the tourist office and have an orange juice and tonic before heading back.

From my hotel is just a short walk to the monster Leclerc supermarket, where I buy a brush for cleaning mud off my boots for the return trip and presents for Scharlie and some local vacuum-packed cured meat. Then I spend an hour in the pool and jacuzzi before an early dinner and bed.

*Cafe on seafront Bastia*

# Day 11 I Penti to Moriani Plage (0m)

**Thursday 23 June , 10km, ascent 100m, descent 660m**

I'm away before six and get a train into Bastia aiming to get the 8.27 bus. There are a few people waiting, including a man in his fifties with a full set of brand-new kit from Decathalon. The road out of Bastia is congested and just after the tunnel and Montesori there is a hold up as far as a traffic island at Furiani.

My aim is to retrace my steps and do the final leg of the walk from I Penti to Moriani and the coast. In Moriani I go to the tourist office and they help me order a taxi and I wait in the Casino next door and have a coffee. The taxi driver arrives. She's a pretty young lady with bright pink nails and big earrings. She is a good driver and takes the mountain road fast.

I don't have time to go to the Gite as it's already late and I have to be down for the bus by 3.20. The issue is not to miss the path and go the wrong way and lose time. But the signing is most inconsistent in frequency, sometimes there are lots of signs and then long stretches with none. I find the path from the road

*Chestnut woods and lush green paddocks below I Penti*

*Fording the Buccatoghju river, having thrown my boots and bag across*

*San Nicolao and the sea*

dropping down to the stream. There is a tricky crossing on slippery stones and it's difficult to avoid a dunking. There follows a delightful walk through woods and a second stream, even more difficult than the first, but the path is good and level.

I hurt a tendon in my left leg just above the ankle the day before yesterday on the descent to I Penti, when I caught it on a root that was sticking up out of the path. Now I pull it again, slipping on a rock. I keep walking on it, trying not to limp, reasoning that this will be the best way of getting down. It seems to work. I take a couple of paracetamol and it helps. I come to a stream swollen with recent rain and can't see a way across on steppingstones, so I take off my boots and throw them and my bag across and wade.

The village of San Nicolas must have been very prosperous; there are five story houses and a hotel-restaurant, long closed. It's very hot near the baroque church of San Nicolas and the path follows lanes and through houses with lemon trees and cork oaks to Moriani.

I walk to the sea, take off my boots and walk in up to my calves. I buy an ice cream and sit in an empty restaurant and eat it until it's time to go for the bus. An easy journey back. I shower, swim, sunbathe and then walk to the beach for a salad dinner and beer. There's a schooner sailing to Elba and ferries to

*Castella must have been a prosperous village in the past*

Capri and the French mainland. I climb back up the steps for my last night in the hotel and pack.

*Baroque church of San Nicolao*

*Moriani Plage and the end of the walk*

# Cap Corse

**Friday 24 June**

A delightfully slow start and a leisurely breakfast with freshly pressed orange juice and coffee with hot milk. Check out and walk to the railway and catch the 9.30 train into Bastia. I have a paranoia missing trains, planes and buses and would normally take the earlier train and hang around for an hour or so. This time I feel I'm being brave and cutting it fine, relying on the train being on time and the Nanny Bag left luggage being quick and efficient.

Both train and Nanny Bag work perfectly and I get to the bus on good time. The shuttle seems too small for all the people waiting, but we all manage to get on. Someone has left their new sticks in my seat; the driver takes them. I hope they get them back.

The journey along the splendid rocky coast road takes just over an hour to Macinaggio. I walk to the end of the promenade and start off along the beach and at the last restaurant have a delicious orange presse. The spacious

*Paillote U Padulu, restaurant the beach, Macinaggio*

*Plage de Tamarone, Cap Corse*

*Jelly fish cove*

restaurant is roofed simply with bamboo rods which let a delightful, dappled light and shade play on the surfaces of the tables and the floor. This is the Sentier du Douanier or Customs Officers' Path.

I walk on, bypassing the promontory with its Genoese watchtower, the Tour de l'Agnellu. After a kilometre or so of pleasant shady walking under a canopy of shrubs the path drops down towards a sandy beach. Halfway down I spot a secluded beach in a rocky cove and climb down and strip off. Wading into the clear water I feel a searing pain in my ankle and see that the water is teeming with small, pink jellyfish.

It's difficult walking out to deeper water on the slippery rocks whilst avoiding the jellyfish but I make it and swim for a while in the deliciously warm water, then sunbathe, dress and walked back.

I try various paths to the watchtower until I find the right one. The watch tower must have been important in warning invasion. There's a new communications tower which must also be important for the island. The stone building next to the tower is humming with air conditioners to keep the processors cool and I drop down to the beach and bathe again to cool off. This time it's soft and sandy and easy to wade out.

I walk back to the village and wait where I had been dropped off, having

*Cove below Sentiers des douaniers*

asked the driver where he would stop to pick up passengers. I get talking to a French lady who is here on holiday with a friend for a week. She's from Lille but she was an au pair in Solihull in her youth. I notice that the shuttle is parked across the road and see it pulling out at 3 o'clock and assume that the driver will pull round to stop where I am waiting. Then I see passengers I recognise from this morning and I yell "Stop!" at the top of my voice and he does. So my worst fear of missing the ferry and being left behind is not to be realised.

It's an easy journey back and even easier to collect my bags. Boarding is uneventful. It's a lovely evening and I go on deck to watch our embarkation. There are a group of men in the bows trying to free a jammed winch. It's holding one of the main lines to the dock and can't be freed. The men toss a light line to the man on the dock to help haul in the mooring rope once they have freed it. Have cast off all the other lines the captain nudges the ferry forwards until the mooring rope goes slack and can be freed and hauled in. There is a beautiful light over the water as we head out to sea and round Cap Corse and I linger on deck before going into dinner. An early night comfortable bed and cabin with a window.

*Genoese watchtower, Punta di a Coscia, Cap Corse*

# Journey home

**Saturday 25 June**

The journey home begins with a rather late start so I'm last on the bus which is convenient at the other end when my bag is at the top of the pile. I walk back up the gentle hill through the rough Saint-Lazare quarter. People in the early cafes at the roundabout look poorly used and uncared for. I find a nice cafe at the station and hang out with coffee and croissants till it's time to leave.

It's a five-hour journey through Provence to Lille and I have a healthy lunch at a Bento bar. There is a short walk to Eurostar terminal and a wait.

On the train from King's Cross to Doncaster I meet a man call Hayden who works as a mental health nurse. He asks me what I learnt on my walk. I say I've learnt on all my long walks that if you keep putting one foot in front of another you can go a long way, so even when you are tired, if you keep plodding on you get there and this is a recipe for life. He asks me about Corsica and I tell

*Crew struggle to free mooring line*

him how unspoilt I found it. It is like walking through a wild garden with the villagers so well attuned to the landscape. He tells me about his family, about his mother from Barbados and that he's been to a commemoration in London for a relative. He tells me about his house and shows me photographs of a delightfully modern 60s house with a large, beautiful garden and says that it was their open house this weekend.

I get a text message from Pierre, now back in Paris, saying he'd also gone the wrong way and had continued down to the road, thus missing out much of the last two stages of the walk and that he intends to come back and complete them one day. I'd like to go back to Corsica and do another walk and wonder if I'll get the chance.

*Farewell to Bastia*

# WILD FLOWERS

*Fine-leafed yetch*

*Mallow and Chamomile (Mayweed)*

*Cyclamen*

*Scarlet Pimpernel (Anagallis arvensis)*

*Wild rock-rose (Cistus salvifolius)*

*Hellebore (Euphorbia Helleborus argutifolius)*

*Rambling bellflower (Campanula patula)*

*Asphodels*

# ROUTE MAP

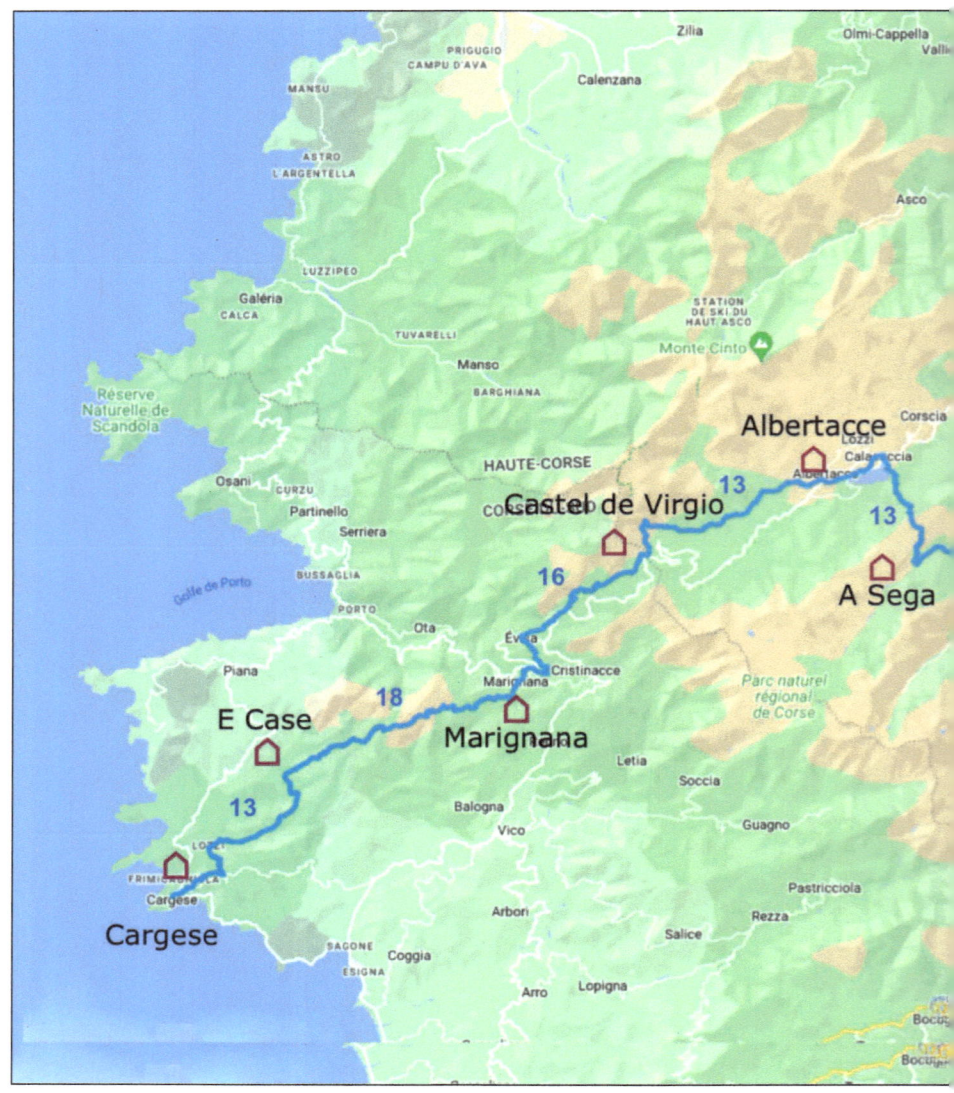

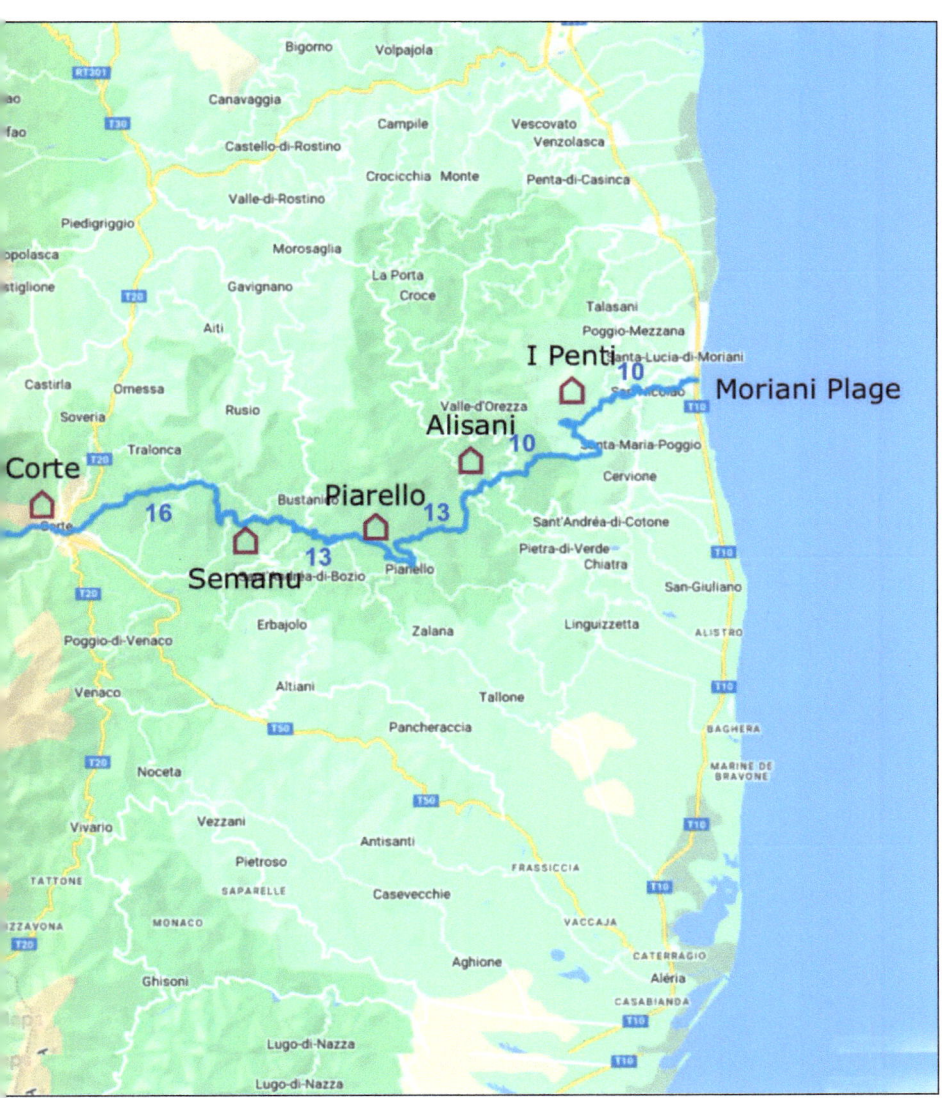

## ITINERARY

| Day | Date | Start | Finish | Km | Miles | Ascent m | Descent | Hrs | Accommodation |
|---|---|---|---|---|---|---|---|---|---|
| Friday | 02-Jun | Home | London | | | | | | |
| Saturday | 03-Jun | London | Cargese | | | | | | Ferry |
| Sunday | 04-Jun | Cargese | E Case | 13 | 8 | 700 | 700 | 5:00 | Hotel le Saint Jean |
| Monday | 05-Jun | E Case | Marignana | 18 | 11 | 930 | 825 | 6:00 | Gîte d'étape ustaria di a Rota |
| Tuesday | 06-Jun | Marignana | Castel de Vergio | 16 | 10 | 880 | 120 | 5:30 | Hotel Castel de Vergio |
| Wednesday | 07-Jun | Castel de Ve | Albertacce | 13 | 8 | 160 | 700 | 4:00 | Gîte d'étape Albertacce |
| Thursday | 08-Jun | Albertacce | A Sega | 13 | 8 | 800 | 450 | 5:25 | Gîte d'étape A Sega |
| Friday | 09-Jun | A Sega | Corte | 13 | 8 | 100 | 770 | 4:25 | Hotel Sampiero Corso |
| Saturday | 10-Jun | Corte | Sermano | 16 | 10 | 1000 | 415 | 5:45 | Gîte d'étape U San Fiurenzu |
| Sunday | 11-Jun | Sermano | Pianello | 13 | 8 | 650 | 650 | 4:45 | Gîte d'étape |
| Monday | 12-Jun | Pianello | Pied d'Alesani | 13 | 8 | 600 | 750 | 4:15 | Gîte d'étape |
| Tuesday | 13-Jun | Pied d'Alesa | I Penti | 10 | 6 | 650 | 530 | 4:00 | Hotel Spa Ostella Montesori |
| Wednesday | 14-Jun | Bastia | Montesorri | | | | | | Hotel Spa Ostella Montesori |
| Thursday | 15-Jun | I Penti | Moriani Plage | 10 | 6 | 100 | 660 | 3:30 | Hotel Spa Ostella Montesori |
| Friday | 16-Jun | Macinaggio | Plage de Tamarone | | | | | | Ferry |
| Saturday | 17-Jun | Bastia | Home | | | | | | |
| TOTAL | | | | 148 | 92 | 6570 | 6570 | 53 | |

# KIT LIST

| Item | Make | Model | Notes | No. | Weight gm | Stars |
|---|---|---|---|---|---|---|
| Rucksack | Lightwave | Fastpac 30 | Excellent, durable but very light. Could do with larger | 1 | 992 | *** |
| Rucksac cover | Lowe | | | 1 | 63 | ** |
| Silk Liner | Sea to Summit | Mummy | | 1 | 138 | *** |
| First aid kit | Boots | | Good, added compeed, second skin, arnica, | 1 | 250 | *** |
| Note book | Moleskin | | I always use these for my journals | 1 | 111 | *** |
| Pens | Biro | | Excellent | 2 | 22 | *** |
| Phone | iPhone | 12 | Good battery life, excellent camera | 1 | 75 | *** |
| Battery/cable | Jackery | 6000 mAh | Not needed | 1 | 176 | ** |
| Head torch | Petzl | Light | and spare battery | 1 | 36 | *** |
| Maps | Didier Richard | Corse du Nord | Excellent, very accurate, durable and easy to use | 2 | 46 | *** |
| Compass | Silva | with whistle | Excellen, very practical, have always used Silva | 1 | 42 | *** |
| Reading glasses | | | | 1 | 22 | *** |
| Pocket knife | Gerber | Paraframe | | 1 | 54 | *** |
| Debit card | | | Essential | 1 | 1 | |
| Dry bags | Sea to Summit | Assorted | Excellent, durable and completely waterproof | 5 | 310 | *** |
| Walking poles | Black Diamond | Distance flz | Excellent, light and well balanced | 2 | 384 | *** |
| Sandals | Clogs | | Useful in camp for tired feet and for getting water fro | 1 | 296 | ** |
| Water bottle | Specialized | | | 1 | 100 | ** |
| Pee bottle | Nalgene 1L | | | 1 | 112 | *** |
| Sun cream | SunSense | Factor 50 | | 1 | 30 | |
| Toothbrush | CuraProX | | | 1 | 25 | |
| Towels | Mountain Warehouse | Ex Large | Plus mini Go face towel | 2 | 151 | ** |
| Lenses, spectacles | | | | 1 | 90 | |
| **TOTAL KIT** | | | | | **3,526** | |
| Boots | Meindl | Bhutan | Excellent, especially for wider feet | 1 | 1,964 | *** |
| Boots | Sportiva | | Wide fitting replacement boots bought in Corte | 1 | 890 | *** |
| Gaiters | Sea to Summit | | Good, light | 1 | 110 | ** |
| Anorak | Arcteryx | Alpha SV | Orange | 1 | 506 | *** |
| Fleece | Berghaus | | Windproof with hood | 1 | 518 | *** |
| Cap | Jack Wills | | Couldn't find favourite North Face cap | 1 | 86 | ** |
| Pants | Kühl | | Excellent, fit well and good pockets | 1 | 351 | *** |
| Shorts | Haglofs | | Excellent, fit well and good pockets | 1 | 299 | *** |
| T shirts | Adidas | | Excellent, stayed looking smart | 3 | 450 | *** |
| Leggings | Lowe | | Gite wear | 1 | 20 | *** |
| Gilet | Mammut | | Emergency wear and used at A Sega Gite | 1 | 415 | |
| Socks | Bridgedale | | Excellent, very comfortable | 2 | 0 | |
| Underpants | M&S | | | 2 | 46 | |
| Swimming trunks | Speedo | | | | 90 | *** |
| Belt | Jukmo | Ratchet belt | Essential, because you loose weight (6-7 kilos) | 1 | 25 | *** |
| **TOTAL CLOTHES** | | | | | **4,880** | |
| **TOTAL** | | | | | **8,406** | |

# TRAINING WALKS

| Date | Title | Area | Distance km | Distance miles | Notes |
|---|---|---|---|---|---|
| 02/10/22 | Chinley Churn & Famine | Hayfield | 6.0 | 3.7 | |
| 13/10/22 | Shining Tor | Goyt Valley | 6.9 | 4.3 | |
| 30/11/22 | White Holme Moss | Ripponden M62 | 16.0 | 9.9 | |
| 01/12/22 | Blackstone Edge | Ripponden M62 | 12.0 | 7.5 | |
| 09/12/22 | Margery Hill from Fairholme | Howden Moors | 20.0 | 12.4 | |
| 15/12/22 | Back Tor from Strines | Howden Moors | 12.0 | 7.5 | Snow |
| 16/12/22 | Stanage | Eastern Moors | 6.0 | 3.7 | Snow |
| 29/12/22 | Alport Castles | Snake | 10.0 | 6.2 | |
| 02/01/23 | High Brown Knoll & Midgley Moor | Hebden Bridge | 15.0 | 9.3 | |
| 04/01/23 | Stanage | Eastern Moors | 8.0 | 5.0 | |
| 06/01/23 | Bamford Edge | Hope Valley | 8.0 | 5.0 | |
| 21/01/23 | Abney Moor | Hope Valley | 4.0 | 2.5 | |
| 02/02/23 | Shatton Moor | Hope Valley | 10.0 | 6.2 | |
| 11/03/23 | Stanage | Eastern Moors | 7.0 | 4.3 | Snow |
| 26/03/23 | Kinder | Kinder | 19.0 | 11.8 | |
| 07/04/23 | Eyam Moor & Bretton Clough | Hope Valley | 11.3 | 7.0 | |
| 14/05/23 | Titchwell | N Norfolk | 6.0 | 3.7 | Bird Club meet |
| 15/05/23 | Wild Ken Hill | Hunstanton | 9.0 | 5.6 | Rewilding / conservation |
| 23/05/23 | Derwent Edge | Derwent Dams | 9.0 | 5.6 | |
| 25/05/23 | Frogatt Edge & White Edge | Eastern Moors | 9.0 | 5.6 | |
| 26/05/23 | Black Hill & Laddow from Crowden | Holme Moss | 20.0 | 12.4 | |
| 29/05/23 | Burgage Round | Eastern Moors | 11.0 | 6.8 | |

# TRAINING WALK PHOTOS

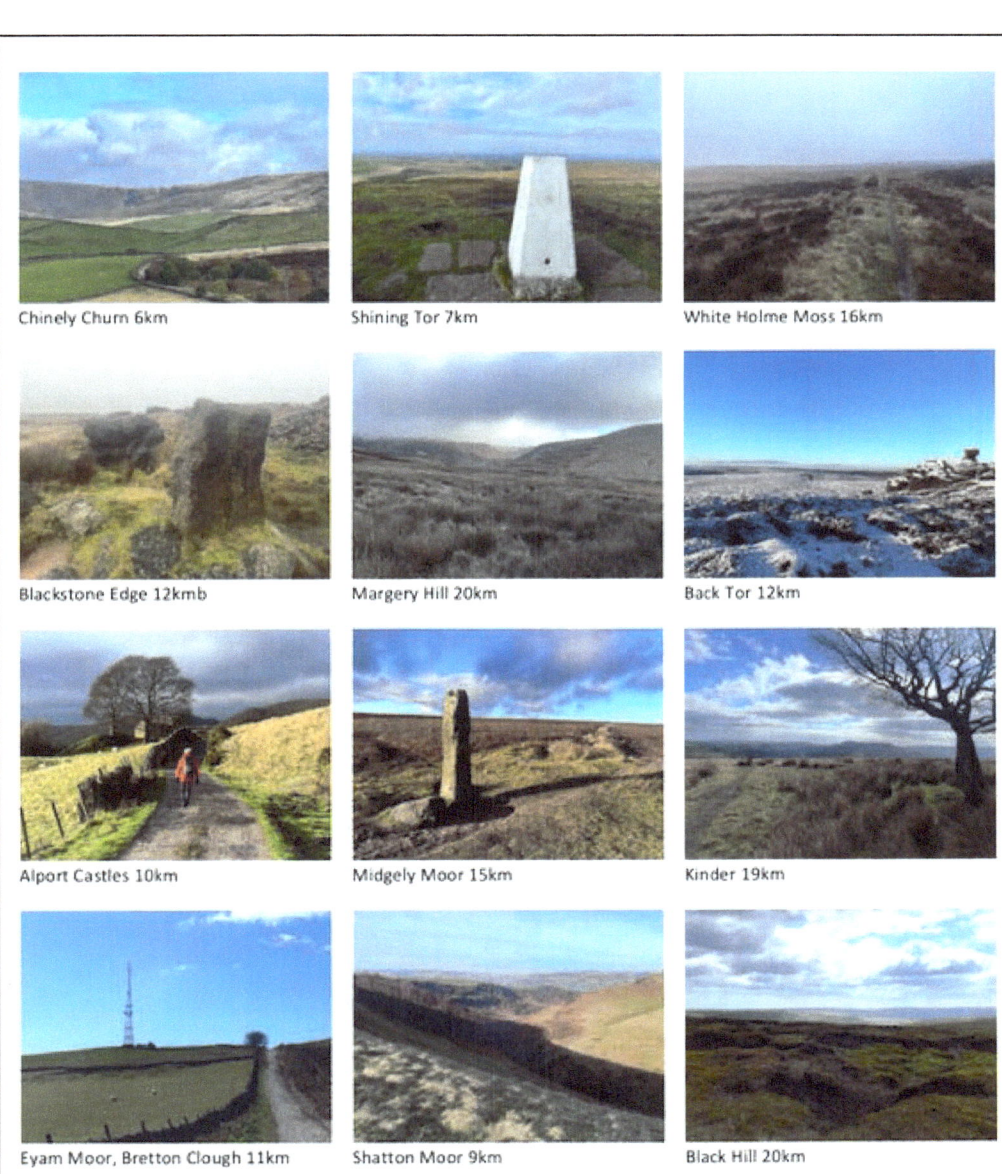

# GEOLOGICAL MAP OF CORSICA

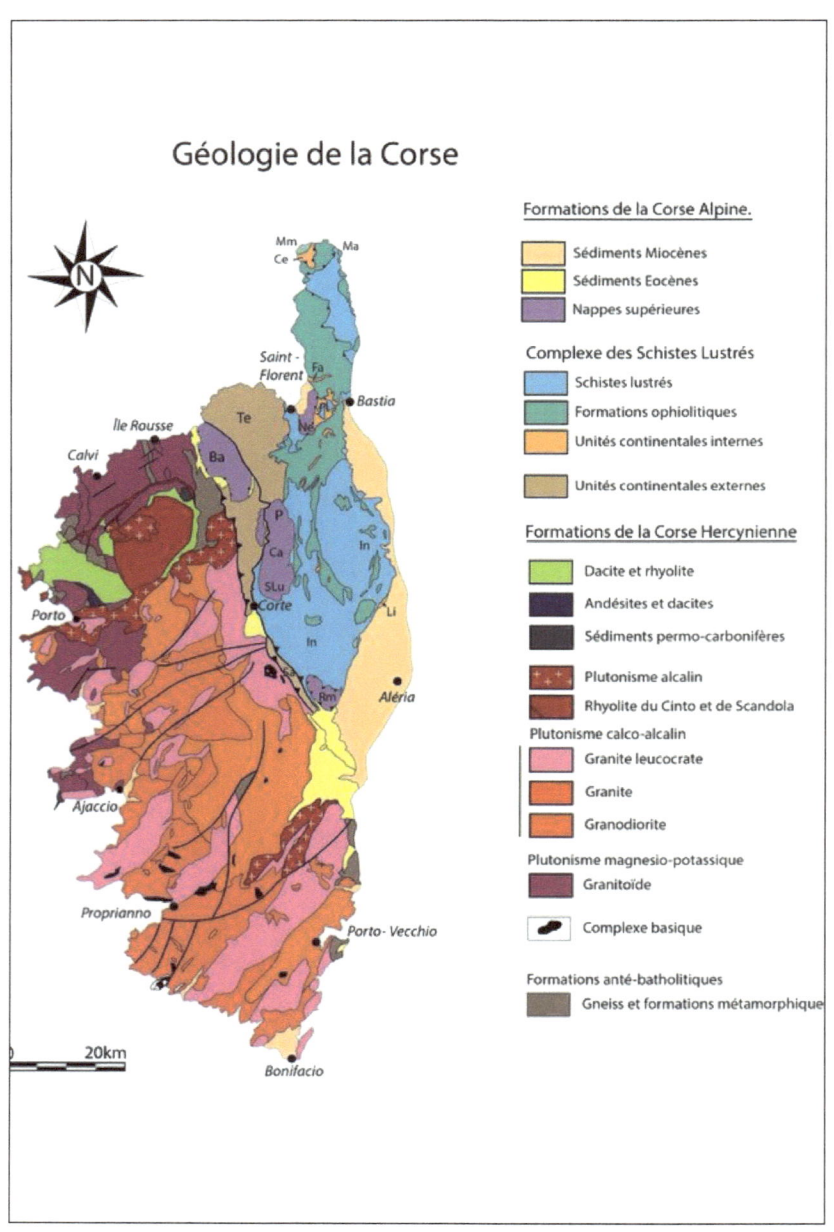

www.ingramcontent.com/pod-product-compliance
Lightning Source LLC
Chambersburg PA
CBHW041607220426
43666CB00001B/8